# MY READING

The Nobel Lecture
and Other Writings

Abdulrazak
Gurnah

BLOOMSBURY PUBLISHING
LONDON · OXFORD · NEW YORK · NEW DELHI · SYDNEY

BLOOMSBURY PUBLISHING
Bloomsbury Publishing Plc
50 Bedford Square, London, WC1B 3DP, UK
29 Earlsfort Terrace, Dublin 2, Ireland

BLOOMSBURY, BLOOMSBURY PUBLISHING and the Diana
logo are trademarks of Bloomsbury Publishing Plc

First published in Great Britain, 2022

A catalogue record for this book is available from the British Library

ISBN: PB: 978-1-5266-5989-7; eBook: 978-1-5266-5988-0;
ePDF: 978-1-5266-5987-3

2 4 6 8 10 9 7 5 3 1

Typeset by Newgen KnowledgeWorks Pvt. Ltd., Chennai, India
Printed and bound in Great Britain by CPI Group (UK) Ltd, Croydon CR0 4YY

To find out more about our authors and books visit www.bloomsbury.com
and sign up for our newsletters

# CONTENTS

# WRITING

## The 2021 Nobel Lecture in Literature

Writing has always been a pleasure. Even as a boy at school, I looked forward to the class set aside for writing a story, or whatever our teachers thought would interest us, more than to any other class on the timetable. Then everyone would fall silent, leaning over their desks to retrieve something worth reporting from memory and imagination. In these youthful efforts, there was no desire to say something in particular, to recall a memorable experience, to express a strongly held opinion or to air a grievance. Nor did these efforts require any other reader than the teacher who prompted them as an exercise in improving our discursive skills. I wrote because I was instructed to write, and because I found such pleasure in the exercise.

Years later, when I was myself a schoolteacher, I was to have this experience in reverse, when

I would sit in a silent classroom while the pupils bent over their work. It reminded me of a poem by D. H. Lawrence which I will now quote a few lines from:

From 'The Best of School'

As I sit on the shores of the class, alone,
Watch the boys in their summer blouses
As they write, their round heads
    busily bowed:
And one after another rouses
His face to look at me,
To ponder very quietly,
As seeing, he does not see.

And then he turns again, with a little, glad
Thrill of his work he turns again from me,
Having found what he wanted, having got
    what was to be had.[1]

The writing class I was speaking of and which this poem recalls, was not writing as it would come to seem later. It was not driven, directed, worked over, reorganised endlessly. In these youthful efforts I wrote in a straight line, so to speak, without much hesitation or correction, with such innocence. I also read with a kind of abandon, similarly without any direction, and

I did not know at the time how closely connected these activities were. Sometimes, when it was not necessary to wake up early for school, I read so late into the night that my father, who was something of an insomniac himself, was forced to come to my room and order me to switch off the light. You could not say to him, even if you dared, that he was still awake and why should you not be, because that was not how you spoke to your father. In any case, he did his insomnia in the dark, with the light switched off so as not to disturb my mother, so the instruction to switch off the light would still have stood.

The writing and reading that came later was orderly compared to the haphazard experience of youth, but it never ceased to be a pleasure and was hardly ever a struggle. Gradually, though, it became a different kind of pleasure. I did not realise this fully until I went to live in England. It was there, in my homesickness and amidst the anguish of a stranger's life, that I began to reflect on so much that I had not considered before. It was out of that period, that prolonged period of poverty and alienation, that I began to do a different kind of writing. It became clearer to me that there was something I needed to say, that there was a task to be done, regrets and grievances to be drawn out and considered.

In the first instance, I reflected on what I had left behind in the reckless flight from my home. A profound chaos descended on our lives in the mid-1960s, whose rights and wrongs were obscured by the brutalities that accompanied the changes brought about by the revolution in Zanzibar in 1964: detentions, executions, expulsions, and endless small and large indignities and oppressions. In the midst of these events, and with the mind of an adolescent, it was impossible to think clearly about the historical and future implications of what was happening.

It was only in the early years that I lived in England that I was able to reflect on such issues, to dwell on the ugliness of what we were capable of inflicting on each other, to revisit the lies and delusions with which we had comforted ourselves. Our histories were partial, silent about many cruelties. Our politics was racialised, and led directly to the persecutions that followed the revolution, when fathers were slaughtered in front of their children and daughters were assaulted in front of their mothers. Living in England, far away from these events yet deeply troubled by them in my mind, it may have been that I was less able to resist the power of such memories than if I had been among people who were still living their consequences. But I was

4

also troubled by other memories that were unrelated to these events: cruelties parents inflicted on their children, the way people were denied full expression because of social or gender dogma, the inequalities that tolerated poverty and dependence. These are matters present in all human life and are not exceptional to us, but they are not always on your mind until circumstances require you to be aware of them. I suspect this is one of the burdens of people who have fled from a trauma and find themselves living safely, away from those left behind. Eventually I began to write about some of these reflections, not in an orderly or organised way, not yet, just for the relief of clarifying a little some of the confusions and uncertainties in my mind.

In time, though, it became clear that something deeply unsettling was taking place. A new, simpler history was being constructed, transforming and even obliterating what had happened, restructuring it to suit the verities of the moment. This new and simpler history was not only the inevitable work of the victors, who are always at liberty to construct a narrative of their choice, but it also suited commentators and scholars, and even writers who had no real interest in us, or were viewing us through a frame that agreed with their view of the world, and who required a familiar narrative of racial emancipation and progress.

It became necessary, then, to refuse such a history, one that disregarded the material objects that testified to an earlier time: the buildings, the achievements and the tendernesses that had made life possible. Many years later, I walked through the streets of the town I grew up in, and saw the degradation of things and places and people, who live on, grizzled and toothless, and in fear of losing the memory of the past. It became necessary to make an effort to preserve that memory, to write about what was there, to retrieve the moments and the stories people lived by and through which they understood themselves. It was necessary to write of the persecutions and cruelties which the self-congratulations of our rulers sought to wipe from our memory.

There was also another understanding of history necessary to address, one that became clearer to me when I lived closer to its source in England, clearer than it had been while I was going through my colonised education in Zanzibar. We were, those of our generation, children of colonialism in a way that our parents were not and nor were those who came after us, or at least not in the same way. By that I don't mean that we were alienated from the things our parents valued or that those who came after us were liberated from colonial influence. I mean that we grew up and were educated in that period of high imperial confidence, at least in our parts of the world, when domination disguised its real self in euphemisms and we agreed to the subterfuge. I refer to the period before decolonisation campaigns across the region hit their stride and drew our attention to the depredations of colonial rule. Those who came after us had their post-colonial disappointments and their own self-delusions to comfort them, and perhaps did not see clearly, or in great enough depth, the way in which the colonial encounter had transformed our lives, that our corruptions and misrule were in some measure also part of that colonial legacy.

Some of these matters became clearer to me in England, not because I encountered people who clarified them to me in conversation or in the classroom, but because I gained a better understanding of how someone like me figured in some of their stories of themselves, both in their writing and in casual discourse; in the hilarity that greeted racist jokes on the TV and elsewhere; in the unforced hostility I met in everyday encounters in shops, in offices, on the bus. I could not do anything about that reception, but just as I learned to read with greater understanding, so a desire grew to write – in refusal of the self-assured summaries of people who despised and belittled us.

But writing cannot be just about battling and polemics, however invigorating and comforting that can be. Writing is not about one thing, not about this issue or that, or this concern or another, and since its concern is human life in one way or another, sooner or later cruelty and love and weakness become its subject. I believe that writing also has to show what can be otherwise, what it is that the hard, domineering eye cannot see, what makes people, apparently small in stature, feel assured in themselves, regardless of the disdain of others. So I found it necessary to write about that as well, and to do so truthfully, so that both the ugliness and the virtue come through, and the human being appears out of the simplification and stereotype. When that works, a kind of beauty comes out of it.

And that way of looking makes room for frailty and weakness, for tenderness amid cruelty, and for a capacity for kindness in unlooked-for sources. It is for these reasons that writing has been for me a worthwhile and absorbing part of my life. There are other parts, of course, but they are not our concern on this occasion. A little miraculously, that youthful pleasure in writing that I spoke of at the beginning is still there after all the decades.

Let me end by expressing my deepest gratitude to the Swedish Academy for bestowing this great honour on me and on my work. I am very grateful.

# MARGATE

It was the summer of 1968, my first summer in England. 'Hey Jude' was playing out of the PA over the miniature golf course over which my friend John presided. He was keeping an eye on the youngsters and their dads putting golf balls under lights, all the while talking to me in a steady spate. He loved talking. I had been there all afternoon, and the smells had changed as the air cooled, so that now, by early evening, the aromas of seaside-resort food had lost some of their edge. 'Hey Jude' had been going all afternoon. It had just been released then, and it played on the radio again and again without respite, and no one grumbled. That is my earliest complete memory of Margate, sitting by the toy golf course in the early evening, listening to that music while John chattered away, and I pretended I was not a lonely and homesick teenager a long way from home.

I had not expected England to get so hot. It was a surprise that the sun blazed, that it made me swelter. The painter Turner lived in Margate and is reported to have described the skies over Margate as the loveliest in Europe. I am not sure what a painter of skies would have meant by such a superlative, but the light that afternoon was bright in a hard-edged way which made the horizon draw near. As the air cooled with the breeze from the sea, I wonder that I did not think to compare where I was to Zanzibar. Because I did not. England seemed so alien then, so unlike anything I had known before.

I had met John in Canterbury, where we were both students at the Technical College. He sought me out as we walked out of a class and fell into step beside me, huge next to me. After a moment he told me that he did not like wogs. The word was new to me, although I had no difficulty guessing its general drift. I asked him why and he said because they smelled.

He would not leave me alone after that. He sat beside me in class even if I tried to find a corner to sit by myself. I liked to sit by myself. The railway station where he caught the train to Margate was on the way to my lodgings, and at the end of the day's classes he waited for me so we could walk home together. He was my protector against the brawling racist abuse which passed for teasing among the English students. And he invited me to Margate and to his home, where his parents fed me and spoke to me politely. They invited me out of curiosity, they said, because John had reassured them that I was not like other immigrants, that I was civilised. I don't know how John arrived at this, but I was not civilised enough that his parents neglected to tell me how much better off I would have been had I stayed wherever I came from. It was not unheard of in 1968, in the England I knew, to be spoken to as shamelessly as this to your face, as if you were without feelings. I lost John at some point. He joined the army and disappeared.

John was not my only link with Margate in those days. Most of the students I knew came from elsewhere – several from the oil countries: Iran, Saudi Arabia, Kuwait. For some reason, they liked to live in Margate. Perhaps they had first arrived there when they came to England. Crowds of students from Europe and from the Middle East came to seaside resorts to learn English, using up the otherwise empty accommodation outside the holiday season. Something about the brash gaiety of the town must have appealed, and several of the students stayed on while they continued studying in Canterbury.

Margate seemed alien when I first knew it, because I had not known about this England. When I arrived in Canterbury, on the other hand, the town was recognisable, familiar from what I had read: the cathedral, the river, the beamed houses; the butcher, the baker and the policeman. Margate was noisy and crowded with people finding pleasure in trinkety games and loud pop music, a place where bands of youths fought incomprehensible battles on the promenade. Margate was Dreamland, from where, every Monday morning at college, came stories of frenzies and seductions, of escapades with the one-armed bandits and the excesses of pop concerts. Sometimes there were stories of mini-orgies, of young women who agreed to have sex with several of my wealthy fellow students.

They blazed with arrogance, the moneybags students, especially the Iranians, who carried themselves with the same assurance that the Shah adopted in the royal photos. For this was still in the days of the Shah, who was known for his global ambitions, so he would perhaps have been pleased that some of his subjects had taken charge of a small corner of Margate and were seducing young women at will. Their bragging tales made their lives in Margate sound lively and full compared to my poverty-stricken struggles in a stuffy lodging house. They made Margate sound dangerous, and gave it a kind of tatty and unattractive glamour.

It was nearly thirty years after that 1968 memory that I visited Margate again. I left the area for several years, and when I returned, it was to live a different life of work and family, and Margate, though only thirty miles away, did not figure in it. In 1997 I went to Margate to record interviews with Czech Roma asylum seekers. They had appeared in Dover in their scores after a TV programme aired in the Czech Republic had depicted the port as a paradise of tolerance and relaxed immigration procedures. Ferry-loads of asylum seekers were turned back, but they came again, bringing others with them. And since they had a case for requesting asylum, suffering persecution in the Czech Republic, in the end several of them were allowed to stay. Margate, just down the road from Dover, got to take several of the refugees.

The Roma asylum seekers spoke about harassment in the Czech Republic, about violence from local youth, how their children were attacked and how the authorities did nothing to protect them. One young woman showed me a mouthful of shattered teeth, the result of an assault with a baseball bat. They spoke about revenge attacks their men undertook, which got them into even further trouble. Then they saw a TV programme which said that Dover was a Roma heaven, where families were given housing, children sent to school, and abusers put in jail, and so they came.

I think I expected more canniness, more cynicism, more worldliness. I think I expected them to be more distraught and angry about their reception. Instead they spoke about the kindness with which they had been treated, about how happy they were to be here, about how good it was to be in a country that was a monarchy (because republics are dictatorships – such ironies!), about how good it felt to be free. It was mostly the women who did the talking. Some of the men were detained in prison in Chatham and Dover, some had already disappeared, and the ones who were there during my conversations sat back watchfully, listening but not saying much. The women talked, describing their anguishes, showing their bruises, while their children clung to them or watched with wide-open eyes. Fighting for their new lives.

By 1997 Margate had collapsed as a seaside holiday resort. The credit boom brought in by Mrs Thatcher's government made any fantasy destination possible. Who would choose Margate, given that option? And the students of English had also gone. The Islamic Republic of Iran preferred to use its money differently, and it was cheaper to purchase half a dozen English teachers and take them to Riyadh than to send a crowd of youths to Margate, where they would pick up strange ways. So the asylum seekers and refugees, and the government money they brought, were welcome when they turned up.

The issue released the vilest xenophobia in the local press ('This Human Sewage' ran one headline). The frenzy reminded me of the time I arrived in England, when something similar was happening about the arrival of Kenyan Asians. So in 1997 I drove along the Margate Promenade, past the harbour, and realised that although it had been an age since I was last here, the memory of its old self was still alive. The Promenade was almost empty, the PA silent and the funfair closed down, and even Dreamland shut after fire damage. That part of town had turned into an abandoned site, not derelict but empty, underused, dangerous, an open detention centre and a hostel for displaced people. The asylum seekers' lives are tense with insecurity, local resentment finds expression somehow, in fights, in vandalism and abuse. It is not quite an asylum-seekers' gulag, but it looks a wreck, living up to its reputation as a decaying town.

# LEARNING TO READ

Then I felt like some watcher of the skies
When a new planet swims into his ken;
Or like stout Cortez, when with eagle eyes
He star'd at the Pacific – and all his men
Looked at each other in wild surmise –
Silent, upon a peak in Darien.
> (John Keats, 'On First Looking
> Into Chapman's Homer')[1]

I begin with those lines from Keats because in some sense they express one dimension of a historical understanding of the world. The poem celebrates the joy of discovering Homer, of discovering new knowledge, and this act is compared to, in the first place, the discovery of Uranus in 1781, a new world in the sky and the first new planet unknown to classical astronomers. It is also compared to Cortez's first sight of the Pacific, although in fact it was Vasco Núñez de Balboa who was the first Spanish commander to see the great ocean. This moment of knowledge is constructed as another instance of human curiosity and human endeavour pushing against stasis and ignorance, and being rewarded by a moment of transcendence. And if it is a moment of fulfilment, it is also one of awed celebration, as we see in that final line of the poem: 'Silent, upon a peak in Darien.' Balboa's recorded reaction was not as awed as Keats would have it and somewhat more enthusiastic and calculating:

> As soon as he beheld the South Sea stretch-
> ing in endless prospect below him, he fell
> on his knees, and lifting up his hands to
> Heaven, returned thanks to God, who had
> conducted him to a discovery so beneficial
> to his country, and so honourable to himself.
> His followers, observing his transports of
> joy, rushed forward to join in his wonder,
> exultation, and gratitude.[2]

In Keats's reading, the poet finds his voice in tribute to a great poet (it was the first poem Keats published and, in a sense, it celebrates poetry) while the soldier Cortez – the brutal conqueror of Mexico – is moved to silence. The acts of knowledge being analogised here might seem at first inappropriate: the poet reading

Homer for the first time and Cortez's mastering gaze on the Pacific. Reading Homer is its own consequence, a completion of an idealised and innocent engagement with the poem, innocent because it need not lead to anything else. Fulfilment lies in the engagement itself. Cortez's 'eagle eyes', as we well know, express a wholly different desire to plunder, possess and subdue. That these two moments are comparable expresses the manner in which the European literary imagination has been able to represent the objects of such greedy 'surmise' as passive, deserving, almost inevitable volunteers to progress.

The point I am making is not a complex one. These two moments are comparable to Keats because they are both instants of revelation, ends in themselves, despite the consequences that await the object of Cortez's gaze. Where you would have expected a logical crisis because of the moral imbalance between these two acts – the pleasure of discovering a great poet on the one hand, and Cortez's chilling anticipation of future conquest on the other – to John Keats there is no dilemma. The plundered victims, their transformations and subjugations, their broken societies are absent from this conception of Europe's advance into the world. It would take

21

us too far away from our subject to illustrate the point with further examples, but I would like to suggest that this conception is not unique to Keats. And where such broken societies are present in a vision of the world, they are present as metaphors of decline and degeneration, or as sites where dilemmas of European sensibility are played out.

The question I would like to turn to now is what such a cultural vision might mean to a reader from outside Europe. And if such a reader were also a writer, how would he or she locate himself or herself in relation to such European writing?

Narratives have their own logic, and as with the imagined gaze of Cortez across the Pacific, they can seem innocent of their consequences, can seem like ends in themselves. This may happen as a result of the narrative's inner compulsion, the powerful tension of the narrative itself, or because the consumer of the narrative unselfconsciously decontextualises its cultural and historical dimensions, or wilfully misunderstands it in order to be able to consume it. I remember packed Saturday-morning cinemas in Zanzibar when I was a child, all of us laughing and cheering as Tarzan outwitted and outfought yet another greasy African nasty, and then yahooed off through the trees with his fresh-faced blonde companion. Everyone in that cinema looked more like the villains than the hero, yet there seemed no contradiction in that identification with Tarzan, just as there seemed none in applauding the slaughter and rout of Muslims, Indians or Native Americans on the cinema screens or in the comics we used to devour.

The Saint Lucian poet Derek Walcott brilliantly captures this sense of implication in the coloniser's narrative in these lines from his long poem *Another Life*:

Cramming half-heartedly for the
　　Scholarship,
I looked up from my red-jacketed
　　Williamson's
*History of the British Empire*, towards
the barracks' plumed, imperial
　　hillsides
where cannon-bursts of bamboo sprayed
　　the ridge,
riding to Khartoum, Rorke's Drift,
through dervishes of dust,
behind the chevroned jalousies
I butchered fellaheen, thuggees,
　　Mamelukes, wogs.[3]

I recognise this sense of seeing oneself through the eyes of another culture, and one which is used to despising you. Most of what we read described the doings of Europeans in the world – explorers, scientists, historians, legions of Cortezes staring with eagle eyes across open seas. The histories we read, though they were delivered with authority, were too self-flattering to be true – and what we read as literature was clearly not meant for us, even if at times we figured in these stories in the way that I alluded to above. And before I could learn to read these texts and see what was there, I first had to learn to look at myself through different eyes, to imagine myself differently as a consumer of these narratives.

I wish I could say that this learning came dramatically, that there was a moment when I picked up a copy of V. S. Naipaul's *The Mystic Masseur* and read for the first time about people I recognised, or that a teacher back from his travels brought with him a copy of James Baldwin's *Another Country* and that reading it made the most profound impression on me. All that would be true, but it would be to give a false idea of the complex and affiliated discourses that such texts invited me to challenge. But if I can't say that there was a dramatic afternoon in August

when I began to read part of my own story in
the world – in history and in literature – then it
is certainly an accumulation of such moments
that made such knowledge possible.

But, in fact, there was an earlier moment than
this which I knew of all along. My encounter with
Kiswahili was as a native speaker, born into it in
our house in Malindi. Many people in Malindi
spoke a smattering of Arabic as well, and some
spoke it fluently. My father was a fluent speaker;
my mother could not speak a word. From other
houses you could hear the sound of Kutchi or
Somali, or the inflexions of Kingazidja. At the
age of five, I was sent to Koran school in Msikiti
Barza, where we were taught to read Arabic
script in order to be able to read the Koran, of
course. I remember our first day, sitting cross-
legged on the floor with several others while a
teenager at a blackboard pointed with his stick
and made us repeat *alif, be, te* after him. A few
months after that, I was sent to Darajani School,
where the first class consisted of learning the
roman alphabet. I already knew the alphabet,
although I can't remember how that came
about, because my father could not read in the
roman alphabet, and my mother could not read
at all at that time. The teacher made me read the
alphabet backwards, because he wanted to make

sure that I had not just memorised it. I mention these complex beginnings as a way of saying that the grip of that cultural vision I began with was not as complete as might first seem, and the co-existence of contradictory cultural traditions felt negotiable.

My encounter with English, then, and for many years after, was casual and instrumental; it was a subject at school. It was not until much later that it had any narrative utility, and could tell me things I was capable of understanding and reflecting on. By that time, I had already been exposed to complex narrative traditions in the Koran school, in commentaries on the Koran, in the Maulid and in qaṣīdas. I had listened to stories at home, told by grannies and aunties. I had heard ribald and forbidden stories in the streets. I cannot describe to you what a rich and unforgettable body of work all this amounted to. Beginning to read with some purpose in English was an encounter with another narrative tradition, and not necessarily a polarising one. What I mean by this is that there was no impossible conflict in partaking in all the different traditions, in addition to, I might add, in listening to tarab, Indian songs and Elvis Presley.

When I think back to that time as a child, it seems to me that there were many more possibilities of making narrative available than I realised. Our own cultural diffidence allowed us to be satisfied with the pleasures of tarab and the Maulid and halwa, and the demands of our colonial education displaced the possibilities I referred to a moment ago. We had to pass examinations, and they were in English, and so, as we proceeded, we were drawn deeper into English and further away from other, more familiar traditions. Where before we learned to memorise qaṣīdas, later we learned to memorise Shakespeare sonnets.

I did some writing while still a schoolboy in Zanzibar. Those efforts were unselfconscious, joyful and playful tasks. I could only think of writing as this occasional activity, and it never occurred to me to try my hand at it except in this frivolous way. I never thought of myself as someone aspiring to be a writer and I don't think I knew of anyone else who had such an ambition.

I was already living and working in England when I began to write differently. In England I was able to read widely and, slowly, English came to me to seem spacious, roomy and hospitable. It was there too that I came to have a sense of the value of writing. I believe that writers come to writing through reading, that it is out of the process of accumulation and accretion, of echoes and repetition, that they fashion a register which enables them to write. I began to write in the bitterness of the experience of those years in England, and I was not concerned with who would read what I wrote or where. I was conscious of being alien and of what choices that put before me, both intellectually and personally. I knew also that this condition was not a contingent of individual circumstances, that a whole discourse existed to describe me, and that I was more or less powerless to resist it. It is partly from this consciousness that I have been interested in the history of how cultures accommodate the contradictions in ideas and in individuals within them.

Novels are complex objects, and it is not always possible to simplify what it is they do, to make them speak in one clear way when circumstances seem to invite such a summary. Having said that, I will still go ahead and make such a summary, knowing that it will be an inadequate expression of what I might say interests me in writing. In other words, it will be an attempt to bring to resolution some of the issues I have been discussing. I have strong convictions about what seem to me the completely destructive narratives of Europe, many of them related to an advance of European imperialism. I think these accounts, which have been with us for three or so centuries, have progressively made beasts and subhumans of the rest of the world, constructed them that way. Many of the things that we say and do now about the world are consequences of these stories that have simply bedded themselves down into history. I want to do what I can to show how demonstrably false these stories are, just as much as I would want to resist the lies of any other culture. I do not mean that to sound like the final word on what I do, but that ambition matters to me. It also matters to me that fiction should engage and dazzle, and give pleasure and pain, and aspire to truth. It is that capacity that writing has to make us see the familiar in an unfamiliar way which makes possible the challenge to apparent truths, a capacity which John Keats too was celebrating with that invocation of Cortez's fierce gaze across the Pacific.

# Indian Ocean Journeys

Amitav Ghosh's 1992 book *In an Antique Land* is an account of a year he spent in a village called Lataifa in Upper Egypt learning Arabic. He called the village Lataifa in the book, although that was not its real name. This was in the mid-1980s, when Ghosh was doing a Ph.D. in anthropology at Oxford. I am not sure why he wanted to learn the Arabic spoken in an Upper Egyptian village, and he does not tell us in his book.

The other narrative line in Ghosh's book concerns the story of a Jewish merchant named Abraham Ben Yiju, who was born in the Maghreb in the early twelfth century, and lived most of his adult life in Aden in southern Arabia and in Mangalore in western India. Ben Yiju's origins were in a region known as Ifriqiya, from the port town of Mahdia in modern-day Tunisia. When he was old enough, Ben Yiju moved to Fustat in Egypt, which was then at one of its peaks of prosperity, where he joined the congregation of the synagogue of Ben Ezra, where many other merchants from Ifriqiya also prayed.

After Fustat, Ben Yiju went to Aden, where he lived for several years, perhaps ten or so, before he moved to Mangalore in India, where he spent at least twenty years, and married and raised children.

Over a long period of time, the Jewish merchants of Fustat, including those of Ben Ezra, were an important part of the trade between the Mediterranean and the Indian Ocean, travelling between Europe, Africa and Asia. Ghosh tells us: 'The vast majority of them were traders, and while some of them were wealthy and successful, they were not, by any means, amongst the most powerful merchants of their time – most of them were small traders running small family businesses.'[1]

We see here the beginnings of an argument that will become important to this text: how closely the Mediterranean was linked to the Indian Ocean trade and how both were paradigms for the inter-penetrability of cultures.

But the synagogue of Ben Ezra was also remarkable for another reason. To prevent the accidental desecration of the name of God, many Jewish communities in the Middle East had a store attached to the synagogue where any writing that mentioned the name of God was kept until the store could be emptied and the documents ritually disposed of, which was done by burying them. The store was called a geniza, and Ben Ezra had one too, constructed when the synagogue was rebuilt in 1025CE. Only, for some reason, the geniza of Ben Ezra was never emptied. For the next nine centuries, through the ebbing and flowing of Fustat's prosperity, through the Muslim conquest in 641CE and the founding of Cairo in 969CE, through Fustat's eventual absorption into that great city and its literal transformation into a rubbish dump, the two-and-a-half-storey-high geniza filled up with papers and, later, books. What is thought to be the last document deposited in the geniza of Ben Ezra was a divorce settlement agreed in Bombay and dated 1875. Ben Yiju is known to us because letters by him and to him were found in the geniza of Ben Ezra some 700 years after they were written and discarded, some no more than scraps of paper which had been reused to do accounts or make lists.

Ghosh describes how he came across the story of Ben Yiju when he was browsing in an Oxford library as a student, and how the story lingered with him until he came to investigate it many years later, after his return from Lataifa. He first read about Ben Yiju in a book called *Letters of Medieval Jewish Traders*, translated and edited by S. D. Goitein (1973). Goitein refers to a letter by a Jewish merchant in Aden, Khalaf ibn Ishaq, to Ben Yiju in Mangalore. Goitein dated the letter as 1139CE. Despite the fact that the Crusades were raging, which were soon to lead to the burning down of Fustat, the letter is businesslike, lamenting the loss of merchandise in a shipwreck and itemising goods received and sent, and not a word about the Christian siege of Damascus or the ever-imminent crusader invasion. Towards the end of the letter there are the greetings to Ben Yiju's family and to his slave. There is also a footnote by Goitein which describes the slave as Indian and a 'business agent, a respected member of [Ben Yiju's] household'.[2]

But Goitein was not the first scholar to draw attention to Ben Yiju's Indian slave. He was preceded by an earlier mention in an article in 1942 by E. Strauss ('New Sources for the History of Middle Eastern Jews', *Zion*, 1942), which referred to another letter from Khalaf ibn Ishaq in Aden to Abraham Ben Yiju in Mangalore, estimated date 1148CE. Aden, as

Ghosh tells us, 'served as one of the principal conduits in the flow of trade between the Mediterranean and the Indian Ocean'.[3] A wide network of Jewish merchants lived there and kept each other informed, and made sure that the valuable information they possessed was kept to themselves. Khalaf ibn Ishaq's 1148 letter, like the 1139 one, also only remarks on small matters of business and family news, and also sends affectionate greetings for the slave of Ben Yiju. These then are the elements that would have lingered for Ghosh, the interconnectedness of the Mediterranean to the Indian Ocean, and the Indian slave who is 'a respected member of the household' and who is remembered so affectionately in Khalaf ibn Ishaq's letters. The mystery in the narrative is to identify the Indian slave, and by the time Ghosh thinks he has done so, a different argument about the interpenetrability of the Mediterranean and the Indian Ocean has been established and the outcome of the quest has receded into the background.

The first mention of the Ben Ezra geniza in European writing was in 1752, when a German traveller looked around the geniza and mentioned it in his travelogue. He saw nothing remarkable in it, but by then the Indian Ocean trade which had been so important to the congregation of Ben Ezra and to the prosperity of Fustat and the wider Mediterranean no longer existed. What trade there was in the Indian Ocean was controlled by European empires.

The next we hear about the geniza is in 1864. It is worth noting that the Suez Canal was built between 1859 and 1869, and during this period Egypt came to figure a little more prominently than usual in the European gaze. Museums and collectors were eager for antiquities, and the genizas of Middle Eastern synagogues were one source. A collector of Jewish antiquities by the name of Jacob Saphir tried to gain entrance into the Ben Ezra geniza, and after considerable persistence was allowed to do so. He found a pile of papers two storeys high, strewn with rubble, because the geniza was open to the skies. He took away a few fragments, which turned out to be of no value as antiquities.

Elkan N. Adler, a British Jew, visited Cairo in 1888. The synagogue of Ben Ezra was demolished soon after Adler's visit, and it was through his influence that the bulk of the geniza documents ended up in the library of the University of Cambridge. The dispersal of the contents of the geniza to libraries in Europe and the United States began then. The story of the dispersal is complicated and at times shocking, but we cannot deal with it here. By the end of the First World War, not a scrap of the geniza documents was left in Cairo.

Why does Ghosh spend so much time on this paper trail, which is related at length in the book and which I have briefly summarised? I think in part it is to establish that it can be substantiated. I understand this from my own experience of colonial education, which taught us to be sceptical about our own stories, as if they were fabrications or fantasies. The existence of letters so firmly linking a Tunisian Jew with Mangalore cannot be brushed away as a fairy tale. But there is also another dimension to the connection with India, and that dimension is Ghosh himself.

*In an Antique Land* is a complex book and I mentioned earlier that it has at least two narrative lines. In the foreground is the narrative of the young anthropology student who spends a year in a village in Upper Egypt, learning Arabic. There he learns that as an Indian he is an exotic, whose customs and practices are strange and repulsive – is it true that you worship cows, is it true that you burn your dead, why do you behave in this shameful way? Ghosh makes comedy of this to some extent, putting these cultural misunderstandings alongside the curiosity and friendship with which he is received by many of the villagers. The tone of this narrative is patient, put-upon comedy, at times the travel writer's self-pity, at other times the respectful anthropology student. But the relentlessness of this reifying questioning also marks and consolidates his marginalisation, and at the same time affirms his affiliation with India.

This estrangement is dramatised in the encounter that the narrator has with one of the learned men of the village, the Imam, who publicly berates the narrator for tolerating such backward customs as burning the dead. In exasperation, the narrator responds by saying it is not something he could put a stop to, and a furious shouting argument develops. In the end, both men boast about the guns and bombs and tanks their nations possess. 'Why, in my country we've even had a nuclear explosion. You won't be able to match that even in a hundred years,' Ghosh's Indian narrator declares.

As Ghosh is pulled away from this scene, he reflects: 'I was crushed, as I walked away; it seemed to me that the Imam and I had participated in our own final defeat, in the dissolution of the centuries of dialogue that had linked us: we had demonstrated the irreversible triumph of the language that has usurped all the others in which people discussed their differences.'[4]

The irony of this modern-day estrangement is the narrative that lurks persistently in the background of *In an Antique Land*, the story of Ben Yiju and his Indian slave, a narrative whose main interest to Ghosh is its demonstration of the ancient links between Egypt and India, a link for which there is now no language in common. In his encounter with the Imam, and his exasperation at his mounting marginalisation, Ghosh sees himself as treacherous to an important idea: 'a world of accommodations that I had believed to be still alive, and, in some tiny measure, still retrievable'.[5] What had contributed to the end of that world of accommodations was European imperial supremacy in the Indian Ocean.

Let me now turn to the mappa mundi of Fra Mauro, created between 1448 and 1460.[6] The usual theory is that the map was commissioned by the King of Portugal shortly before 1450, and was produced for him in 1457–59. Recent discoveries in Venetian archives suggest that the Portuguese version was a copy of a map commissioned by the Republic of Venice between 1448 and 1453. The Portuguese copy has been lost, but here is a description of the original

Venetian one, which is held at the Biblioteca Marciana in Venice:

> Nearly six feet in diameter, painted on parchment glued to wood panels ... [t]he circular map is mounted in a heavy square frame hanging in its own room and is usually covered by a curtain to protect it from the light. When the curtain is drawn aside, one sees a rich abundance of colour and detail: ships sailing on seas rippled with blue and white, innumerable tiny castles mounted on hills, rivers winding throughout the land, irregularly shaped islands scattered in the sea. In addition to thousands of place names, the map is covered with two hundred descriptive texts, sometimes mounted on scrolls that are pasted onto the surface.[7]

Fra Mauro lived on one of the islands in the Venetian Lagoon called Murano, and he made his map without stirring from there (although he had a well-travelled collaborator in Andrea Bianco), basing the map on information he collected from other maps, and from informants. The King of Portugal's interest in the map was to do with his state's aggressive search for a route to the Indian Ocean by rounding Africa. To some extent, Fra Mauro's map explores the credibility of this search, when Ptolemy's map proposed that what we now call the Indian Ocean was landlocked.

In defence of his sedentary scholarship, Fra Mauro referred to the people and the many writings he had consulted in the preparation of his map. What were these writings? With reference to the Indian Ocean, these were certainly Arab and Persian sources. The Arabs in particular were the great sailors of the western Indian Ocean, at least in part because the monsoon winds favoured them and gave them a longer sailing season than the south Asians. These could have included the tenth-century contemporary accounts of 'Zingbar' and 'Zangistan'[8] in al-Mas'ūdī's world encyclo-paedia *Murūj al-dhahab* (*The Meadows of Gold*), in which he gives an eyewitness account of travelling to the port of Qanbalu in Pemba. There is also Ibn Hawqal, who reports hearsay on 'Zingbar', and the anonymous geography *Ḥudūd al-ʿĀlam* (*Regions of the World*), which attempts to locate 'Zangistan'. The philosopher Al-Biruni in his *Chronology of Ancient Nations* suggests:

The sea beyond 'Sofala of the Zanj' was impossible to navigate, and no ship which ventured there had ever returned to give an account of what it had seen ... This southern ocean is navigable. It does not form the utmost southern limit of the inhabitable world. On the contrary, the latter stretches still more southward.

Al-Biruni believed specifically that there was a sea route round Africa, linking the Atlantic with the Indian Ocean: 'One has certain proofs of this communication, although one has not been able to confirm it by sight.'[9] Another source for Fra Mauro would have been Jewish merchants, who were able to travel relatively freely between the two religions, as we have seen, although they were secretive about what they knew. Another source which would have been invaluable to Fra Mauro, but which was certainly unknown to him, was the memoirs of the Moroccan traveller Ibn Battuta, whose travelling exploits were not known of in Europe until the nineteenth century, but who between 1325 and 1354 travelled and lived from Fez to Beijing and several cities and regions in between, and from Central Asia and southern Russia to Timbuktu. In 1331 he travelled with the northeast monsoons as far south as Kilwa, stopping on the way in Mogadishu and Mombasa. Then, when the winds changed, he crossed the Indian Ocean to southern Arabia.

In other words, what these sources demonstrate – the geniza letters, the sources I have just mentioned – is that a great deal is known about the Indian Ocean and its archipelago of cultures by the time of Fra Mauro's map. The map, it seems to me, demonstrates, among other things, that the Indian Ocean littoral is represented in its own narrative. Fra Mauro's reports are sketchy, and some are wrong, but what the map demonstrates is an Indian Ocean world of traffic, merchandise and stories.

Then, in the early months of 1498, the real business began: Vasco da Gama's ships entered the Indian Ocean in January of that year and began creeping up the African coast to inaugurate the modern era. By the middle of May, they had reached Calicut on the Malabar coast, piloted there by an 'Arab' from Malindi. They stayed only briefly, offending and being offended, and then sailing off after delivering a farewell broadside on the city. It was to be the first of several as the Portuguese slashed and burned their way across the Indian Ocean for the next hundred years. For the Portuguese quickly realised that there was no contestant to their seaborne military power. Trade across the northern Indian Ocean had never been under the military control of any state, and the shock of Portuguese destruction of all competitors would have seemed like hysterical greed. There is some disagreement about the extent of the militarisation of the Indian Ocean littoral, but here is K. N. Chaudhuri on how it conducted its trade:

> we know that before the arrival of the Portuguese in the Indian Ocean in 1498 there had been no organised attempt by any political power to control the sea-lanes and the long-distance trade of Asia. The Iberians and their north European followers imported a Mediterranean style of warfare by land and sea into an area that had hitherto had quite a different tradition. The Indian Ocean as a whole and its different seas were not dominated by any particular nations or empires.[10]

When Da Gama returned to Calicut in 1502 with a hugely increased force, he made the point about Portuguese supremacy with devastating barbarism: bombarding the town, boarding the ships in the harbour (about twenty) and mutilating the sailors by cutting off noses, ears and hands and sending a boatload of them back to the Samudra-raja, suggesting that he might like to make curry with the pieces, then he set fire to all the captured ships with the mutilated sailors still on board. Such events – towns destroyed, populations mutilated and killed – were to be repeated along the coast of Africa (Kilwa, Mombasa, Pate, Faza), in the Persian Gulf (Muscat, Hormuz) and western India. To the surprised ports and cities along the Indian Ocean coastline it must have seemed as if something demonic and catastrophic had befallen the world.

The familiar way of telling the history of the Indian Ocean for the next 500 years is to focus on the activities and increasing control of the European empires. The frantic and drunken sailors and knights of the Portuguese fleets are soon to be supplanted by the ruthless and orderly Dutch (no booze allowed on their ships), the scheming and grandiose French, whose every plan is undone by the humiliating concession in the next peace treaty, which the competent and ultimately masterful English force on them. The Portuguese rapidly disappear from the picture now. The traveller and translator Richard Burton summarised their defeat in this way: 'above all things, the slow but sure workings of the shortsighted policy of the Portuguese in intermarrying and identifying themselves with Hindoos of the lowest castes, made her fall as rapid as her rise was sudden and prodigious'.[11]

The focus shifted to relations between the three 'modern' European states as they jostled for supremacy in the Indian Ocean, soon to be joined by the Germans.

It had to wait until the evangelical movements in Europe and the exploration mania to reach a peak before writing conventions for representing the African Indian Ocean littoral were established. These included the orientalising of the western Indian Ocean littoral as Arab, backward and addicted to slaves and the harem. The European evangelist and explorer and later government official had come both to restrain the despotic tendencies of the Arabs and also to succour the Africans. Various forms of these conventions can be seen in the memoirs of explorers and bishops, in popular travelogues and in fiction. In some respects, these conventions still survive.

I was born and grew up in Zanzibar. In the part of town where we lived, which was then called Malindi, the dominant narrative was the sea and the ocean beyond it. From the upstairs windows of the house we lived in then, you could see the dockside warehouses and the dhow harbour and beyond that, way out to sea.

Many of the people in that part of town lived by the sea: fishermen, sailors or, less dangerously, merchants who traded the products of the sea. My father was one such merchant, trading mostly in dried and preserved fish, and other products of the Indian Ocean trade, one of Ghosh's small traders. Every year at around November or so, the winds and the currents of the south-west monsoon blow from the Bay of Bengal, across south India and south Arabia, along the Somali coast and all the way to Zanzibar, and every year, when I was a child, they brought with them dozens and dozens – what felt like hundreds – of dhows from across the ocean, laden with goods to trade, and they all ended up in the dhow harbour in our backyard. There were so many dhows and packed so tightly that sometimes we would see the sailors walk from one boat to another across the harbour.

In Ghosh's narrative it is North Africans who travel to India to find a living. When his narrator reaches Mangalore on the tracks of Ben Yiju's Indian slave, he sees the prosperous-looking houses in some of the nearby areas, which were built as a result of remittance money from the Gulf, where so many Indians had gone to find a living. Instead of North Africans and Arabs coming to India to make their fortunes, now

Indians were going to Arab lands to do the same. He sees the Indian presence in the Gulf as a continuation of a 'medieval heritage', but this might seem too optimistic. The journeys, however, continue, and one of the more remarkable manifestations of this is the spread of Kiswahili. Kiswahili means 'the language of the coast', and it is well known that it is now the most widely spoken African language, but is less well known that it is spoken as a first language across the ocean, in Oman and the Gulf cities where whole districts are enclaves of people from the ocean's western shores. But these are only remnants of what was there before, and like Ghosh, I too lament the loss, 'the dissolution of the centuries of dialogue that had linked us'.

# NOTES

## WRITING

1 'The Best of School' from D. H. Lawrence, *The Complete Poems of D. H. Lawrence*, Wordsworth Editions, Ware, 1994, p. 18.

## LEARNING TO READ

1 'On First Looking into Chapman's Homer', The New Oxford Book of English Verse 1250–1950, Chosen and Edited by Helen Gardner, Oxford University Press 1972, p 602.

2 Bernice Slote, 'Of Chapman's Homer and Other Books', *Prairie Schooner*, vol. 55, no. 1/2 (spring/summer 1981), pp. 82–90; Joseph Warren Beach, 'Keats's Realms of Gold', *PMLA: Publications of the Modern Language Association of America*, Cambridge University Press, March 1934, 49 (1), pp. 246–57.

3 Derek Walcott, *Complete Poems 1948–1984* (New York: The Noonday Press, Farrar, Straus & Giroux, 1986) p. 211.

## Indian Ocean Journeys

1 Amitav Ghosh, *In an Antique Land*, Granta Books, London, 1992, p. 56.

2 *Ibid.*, p. 18.

3 *Ibid.*, p. 16.

4 *Ibid.*, p. 236.

5 *Ibid.*, p. 237.

6 Fra Mauro's map appears in black-and-white at the start of 'Indian Ocean Journeys'. It can be found in full colour here: https://www.bridgemanimages.com/en/italian-school/fra-mauro-map-1460-map/map/asset/529889.

7 Evelyn Edson, *The World Map 1300–1492*, Johns Hopkins University Press, Baltimore, Maryland, 2007, p. 141.

8 Ghosh, *In an Antique Land*, p. 37.

9 *Ibid.*, p. 38.

10 K. N. Chaudhuri, *Trade and Civilisation in the Indian Ocean*, Cambridge University Press, Cambridge, 1985, p. 14.

11 Richard Burton, *Goa and the Blue Mountains*, Richard Bentley, London, 1851, p. 45.

# A NOTE ON THE AUTHOR

Abdulrazak Gurnah is the winner of the Nobel Prize in Literature 2021. He is the author of ten novels: *Memory of Departure, Pilgrims Way, Dottie, Paradise* (shortlisted for the Booker Prize and the Whitbread Award), *Admiring Silence, By the Sea* (longlisted for the Booker Prize and shortlisted for the Los Angeles Times Book Award), *Desertion* (shortlisted for the Commonwealth Writers' Prize) *The Last Gift, Gravel Heart* and *Afterlives*, which was shortlisted for the Orwell Prize for Fiction 2021 and longlisted for the Walter Scott Prize. He was Professor of English at the University of Kent. He lives in Canterbury.

# A NOTE ON THE TYPE

The text of this book is set in Linotype Sabon, a typeface named after the type founder, Jacques Sabon. It was designed by Jan Tschichold and jointly developed by Linotype, Monotype and Stempel in response to a need for a typeface to be available in identical form for mechanical hot metal composition and hand composition using foundry type.

Tschichold based his design for Sabon roman on a font engraved by Garamond, and Sabon italic on a font by Granjon. It was first used in 1966 and has proved an enduring modern classic.